No Waste Lunch

No More Waste

Here is my apple.

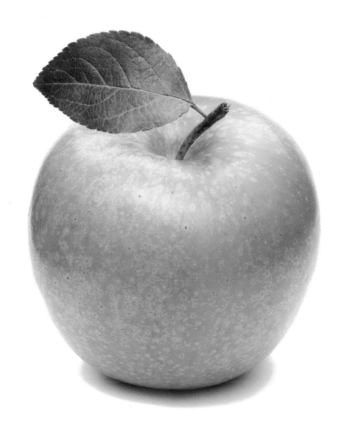

Here is my banana.

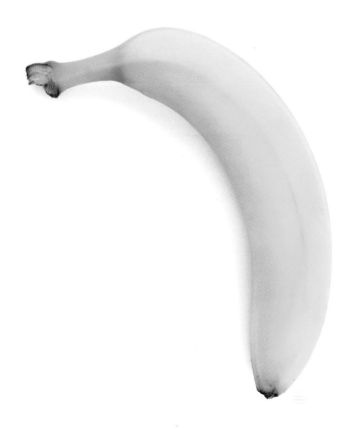

5

Here is my sandwich.

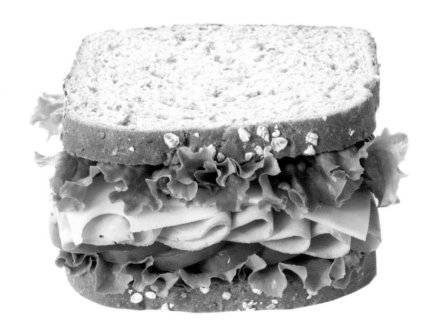

Here is my **sandwich wrap.**

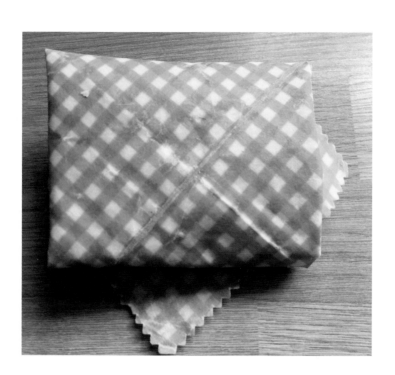

9

Here is my **treat.**

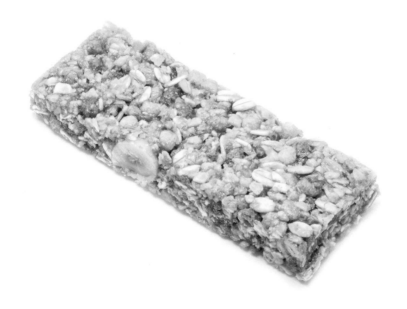

Here is my **lunch bag.**

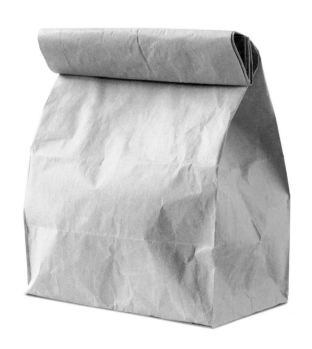

Here is my lunch.

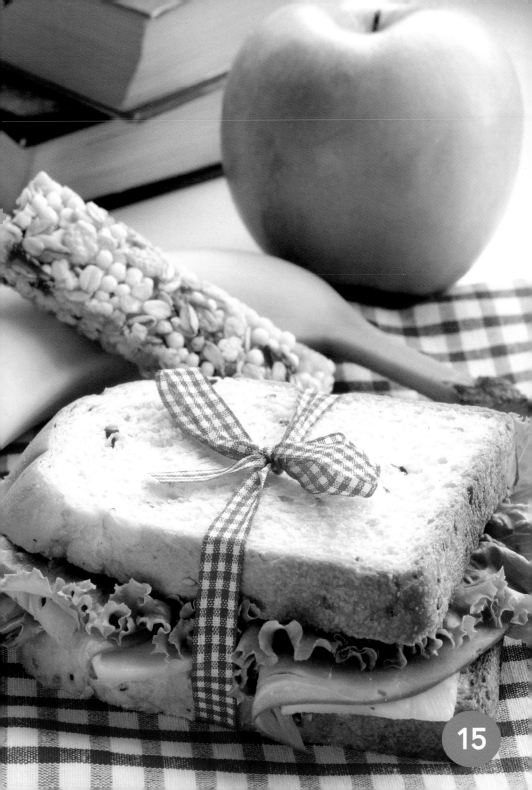

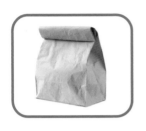 lunch bag

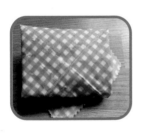 sandwich wrap

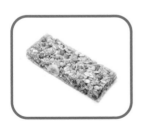 treat